THE NIGHT LIGHT

Modern Curriculum Press
BEGINNING TO READ Series

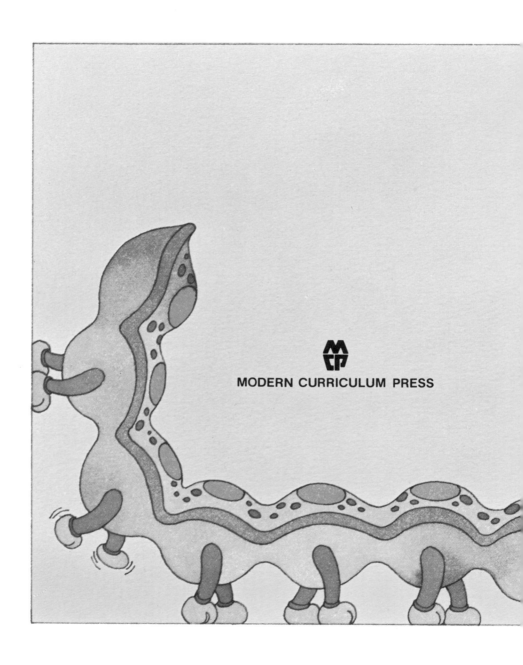

MODERN CURRICULUM PRESS

THE NIGHT LIGHT

Susan Mathias Smith

Illustrated by Terry L. Wickart

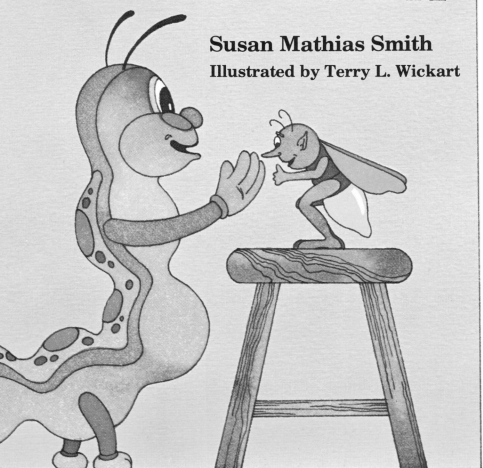

Library of Congress Cataloging in Publication Data

Smith, Susan Mathias.
  The night light.

Summary: Although he is the biggest, bravest, and greenest bug in town, William Green is afraid of the dark.
(1. Fear—Fiction. 2. Night—Fiction)   I. Wickart, Terry L.   II. Title.
PZ7.S65942Ni   (E)   81-4095   AACR2

ISBN 0-8136-5612-5 (Paperback)
ISBN 0-8136-5112-3 (Hardbound)

    7 8 9 10   02 01

William Green was the biggest and the bravest and the greenest bug in all the town. He had the most feet, too.

There was hardly anything that frightened William Green.

William was not afraid of hairy spiders.

William was not afraid of high places.
He was not even afraid of the wind.
When the wind blew hard, William just
hung on tightly.

William was not afraid of deep water.

William was not afraid to go through
tall grass. Sometimes people's feet
tramped on William, but he
wasn't afraid. William just
bent a little.

There was one thing that did frighten William, though. That was the dark.

When night came, William never wanted to go to bed. He always went up the stairs to his room very slowly.

William didn't know why he was afraid.
He only knew that he was afraid.

William was so scared that he hid under the covers on his bed. It was hot under the covers, and William always had a hard time getting to sleep.

William did not like being afraid of the dark, but what could he do about it? He thought and thought and thought.

Finally William had an idea. He decided to catch Flash, the lightning bug that lived down the street. Flash made little blinks of light at night.

William caught Flash and put him in a cage in the bedroom. Flash made a good night light for William. Now William was happy because his room was not dark. He didn't hide under the covers any more.

But Flash was not happy. One night
Flash began to cry. He cried so hard that
he woke up William.

William sat up in bed and looked at
Flash.

"What's wrong?" asked William.

"I want to go home," cried Flash.
"I don't like living in a cage."

William didn't want Flash to cry,
so William said, "You can go."

William let Flash out of the cage.

Then William began to cry.

Flash asked William, "What's wrong with you?"

"Now I'll be afraid of the dark again," William cried.

"No, no," said Flash, "don't be afraid of the dark. The dark won't hurt you."

"How do you know?" asked William. "You have a light that blinks in the dark. I don't have a light. I'm all alone in the dark."

Flash said, "You can have a night light, too. I'll tell you how."

"How?" asked William.

Flash said, "Close your eyes and think of
light, bright things. Think of

white puppies,

orange guppies,

pink lollipops,

and

bright yellow tops."

And with that, Flash flew out the
window. William watched Flash fly to
his home in a garden down the street.

Night came, and William went to bed. He was scared again, but then he remembered what Flash had said.

He closed his eyes and thought of white puppies, orange guppies, pink lollipops, and bright yellow tops.

The room was dark, but inside of
William's head it was light. William
smiled and fell asleep.

And from that night on, William was
never, ever afraid of the dark again.

Susan Mathias Smith is a free-lance writer and teaches English in a high school.

In addition to giving practice with words that most children will recognize, *The Night Light* uses the 24 enrichment words listed below.

bedroom	finally	scared
bent	flew	spiders
blew	frighten(ed)	stairs
blinks		
bug	guppies	tightly
		tramped
caught	hairy	
close(d)	hid	wind
		woke
deep	lightning	wrong
	lollipops	